MW01228578

The Twisted Truth

11 Stories

11 Lies

CAN YOU RELATE?

By

EBONIE "EVE" SMITH

Introduction:

In "The Twisted Truth: 11 Stories 11 Lies", readers are invited to explore the real-life experiences of individuals who have grappled with insecurity, anxiety, and depression to name a few. Inspired by modern societal pressures—especially those amplified by social media—this book exposes the challenges many faces as they navigate a world of curated images and unrealistic expectations. The book's mission is to remind readers that the perfection they see online is often a façade, and that they are enough just as they are.

However, "The Twisted Truth" delves beyond social media, exploring the complexity of relationships and the struggles inherent to them, whether with friends, family, or romantic partners. The book also addresses the impact of discrimination on self-worth and how those affected can rebuild their confidence despite unfair treatment.

Within these pages, readers will encounter stories that highlight not only the pain of prejudice but also the struggles to find acceptance and belonging. By shedding light on these issues, The Twisted Truth aims to build empathy and foster healing, encouraging readers to see that, often, insecurities reflect more about the people projecting them than those who feel them.

This collection invites readers to reflect deeply, offering a pathway to self-acceptance and understanding in the context of today's societal pressures.

Table on contents:

Dedication

To my daughter, Dannah – My love for you is beyond words. You're not only my daughter but my best friend, my light, and my strength in tough times. Thank you for being you.

To my son, David – You're so much like me, and I'll always have your back. From the moment you were born, I knew you were a star. Keep reaching for your dreams. I love you deeply.

To my "Little CEO," Mikey Jr. – You're destined for greatness. Keep shining; you're protected and loved. Your dad is always with you, watching proudly.

To Grandma Susie – I am forever grateful for you. Thank you for your love and guidance.

To my mom, Patricia – You've been like a big sister to me, and I see so much of you in myself. I'm proud of who you've become. Love you always.

To my "Daddy" Thomas – I love you more than words can say.

To my dad – Thank you, OG! If it wasn't for you, I wouldn't be here. You created a monster, and I mean that in the best way! Love you.

To my sister, Niasia – Keep pushing forward. You're strong and capable, and I believe in you always.

To my best friend, Lynese (aka Babs Bunny) – We're locked in for life. Love you, sister.

To Viper – Thank you for the constant encouragement and support. You remind me that there's nothing I can't achieve, as long as I stay focused and keep my mind on the prize. I appreciate having you in my life.

Thank you, Daze, for helping put this together and guiding me in the right direction. I truly appreciate you.

Shout out to Calico – Your motivation helped me write this book. You have no idea the influence you have on others. Keep being that guy and thank you.

Special shout outs to my Ancestors, Yina, Jaja, Enisha, June, Zarina, Bugottii, Tia, Cynthia, Meda, Shamel, Suave, Kimbah, Tammy, Delita, Marshall, Tee Bully, Chris, Lady Keyz, Kamile, Marsha, Nikki, Harold, Olu, Iyalosha Tinubu, – and to anyone I may have missed, my apologies.

I appreciate each of you. Let's keep growing on this journey together.

Love you all! 🖤

Chapter One: The Mirror Lies No More

Monica, a young Black woman, found herself in a seven-year relationship with Johnathan—a man who constantly made her feel small. Though she loved him deeply, she came to realize he only stayed with her because she catered to him in ways that reminded him of his mother's nurturing. But there was a painful truth she couldn't ignore: he wasn't truly attracted to her.

Monica's self-esteem withered as she watched Johnathan live a double life on social media. He never posted photos of them together, yet he proudly shared images of himself with exotic women and even his exes, labeling them as "throwback pics" without regard for Monica's feelings. Unlike his past relationships, where he showcased his love online, he kept Monica hidden, as though she were someone to be ashamed of. He even traveled alone, taking vacations where he would cheat on her with women in different countries.

One day, while using his computer, Monica stumbled across videos that shattered her heart—footage of Johnathan with women from around the world. Her self-worth plunged deeper than she ever thought possible. Johnathan's words echoed in her mind: "Nobody is going to want a woman with kids." He repeatedly suggested that she was lucky to have him, trying to convince her that he was the best she could ever hope for.

Despite his putdowns, Monica clung to the relationship, desperate to hold on to what she thought she had. But the reality was that he offered no real support, especially in the things that meant the most to her. Behind closed doors, Johnathan was a different person—cruel, belittling, and dismissive of her dreams. He had a way of turning on the charm for others, but when they were alone, he revealed his true colors.

For the first time in her life, Monica felt completely defeated. This was a woman who had always carried herself with pride and confidence, but now she felt like a shadow of who she once was. It wasn't until she stood in front of the mirror one day, really looking at herself, that she had a moment of clarity. "What the hell is wrong with you? Look at you, and look at him," she said to her reflection, finally recognizing how much she had given up for someone who didn't deserve her.

They hadn't been intimate in two years—Monica was repelled by the thought of being with him. During that time, she was busy working toward her bachelor's degree, while Johnathan spent his days glued to YouTube, pretending he was learning from "YouTube University." He had no ambition, no high school diploma, and wasted his time gambling. He had nothing going for himself, while Monica was striving for more.

As Monica began to research his behaviors, she stumbled across the term "narcissist." As she read more about it, everything clicked into place. Johnathan's need for validation, his tendency to manipulate her feelings, and his complete lack of empathy were all hallmarks of narcissism. This revelation was a turning point for Monica; she understood that the problem wasn't her. It never was. She was always strong, beautiful, and deserving of real love.

With a newfound determination, Monica decided it was time to take control of her life. The first step was to end her relationship with Johnathan. It wasn't easy; after six years of emotional manipulation and the fear of being alone, Monica felt a tug at her heart as she prepared to say goodbye. But deep down, she knew that the only way to heal was to remove the toxic presence from her life.

One evening, as they sat in silence on the couch, Monica mustered the courage to speak up. "Johnathan, I can't do this anymore. I need to prioritize my happiness, and this relationship isn't bringing me joy. It's holding me back." He looked at her, surprised but quickly shifted into his defensive persona. "You're making a mistake. No one else will want you." But this time, his words bounced off her like water off a duck's back. Monica had finally recognized her worth.

After ending the relationship, Monica threw herself into her studies and personal development. She surrounded herself with supportive friends and family, people who reminded her of her strength and potential. She joined a local women's empowerment group, where she met other women who shared their own stories of overcoming insecurities and challenges. Hearing their experiences inspired her, igniting a fire within her to reclaim her self-esteem.

As Monica continued her education, she began to explore her interests outside of her degree. She took up painting and joined a local book club. With each new activity, she discovered hidden talents and passions she never knew she had. She learned to enjoy her own company, celebrating her achievements, no matter how small she was.

One day, while painting in her living room, Monica caught sight of her reflection in the window. She noticed the sparkle in her eyes and the smile that had returned to her face. It was a stark contrast to the sadness that had once lingered there. She realized she was no longer defined by her past relationships or the hurt she had endured. Instead, she was growing into the woman she had always wanted to be—strong, independent, and unapologetically herself.

In time, she graduated with her bachelor's degree, a milestone that filled her with pride. On the day of her graduation, she stood tall on the stage, beaming with joy as she accepted her diploma. Looking out into the crowd, she spotted her family and friends cheering her on, and for the first time in a long while, she felt truly loved and supported.

Monica also began to date again, but this time, she was cautious. She took her time getting to know potential partners, ensuring that they respected her and appreciated her for who she was. She learned to set boundaries and recognize red flags, refusing to settle for anything less than what she deserved.

Months later, Monica reflected on her journey during a night out with friends. She raised her glass and shared her story—how she had once felt trapped in a toxic relationship but had emerged stronger and more confident. Her friends applauded her bravery, and she felt a wave of gratitude wash over her. She had come so far and had no intention of looking back.

As she left the bar that night, Monica felt a sense of freedom and empowerment that she had never known before. She was ready to embrace the future, knowing that she was worthy of love and happiness. She vowed to keep growing, to continue seeking out new experiences, and to inspire others with her story.

In the end, Monica learned that true love starts from within. She had transformed her pain into power, and she knew she would never let anyone diminish her light again.
Here's a detailed exploration of how Monica heals, incorporating various aspects of her journey toward self-acceptance, emotional recovery, and personal growth:

Monica's Healing Journey

Emotional Acknowledgment: Monica begins her healing process by acknowledging her feelings. After ending her relationship with Johnathan, she allows herself to feel the pain and disappointment. She journals her thoughts, writing down her experiences and emotions, which helps her process the trauma she endured. This act of reflection becomes a therapeutic outlet, giving her a safe space to articulate her feelings.

Seeking Support: Monica recognizes the importance of having a support system. She reaches out to close friends and family, sharing her story and seeking encouragement. Their love and validation help her understand that she is not alone in her struggles. She also finds a therapist who specializes in trauma and emotional abuse, allowing her to unpack her experiences in a safe environment.

Educating Herself: After discovering the term "narcissist," Monica dives deep into understanding narcissistic behavior. She reads books, attends workshops, and participates in support groups focused on healing from toxic relationships. This education empowers her to recognize unhealthy patterns in relationships, reinforcing her resolve to avoid similar situations in the future.

Building Self-esteem: To rebuild her self-esteem, Monica sets small, achievable goals for herself. Whether it's completing a project for school, trying a new hobby, or simply spending a day pampering herself, each accomplishment boosts her confidence. She starts speaking affirmations in the mirror every morning, reminding herself of her worth and capabilities.

Exploring New Passions: Monica embraces creativity as a form of self-expression. She takes up painting and finds solace in the act of creating. Art becomes a powerful tool for her healing, allowing her to convey her emotions and experiences visually. She joins local art classes, meets like-minded individuals, and begins to explore her artistic talents.

Setting Boundaries: Through therapy and self-reflection, Monica learns the importance of setting boundaries. She practices saying no to situations and people that drain her energy or compromise her wellbeing. This newfound assertiveness not only helps her regain control over her life but also cultivates healthier relationships in the future.

Engaging in Self Care: Monica prioritizes selfcare, recognizing that taking care of her physical and mental health is crucial. She establishes a routine that includes regular exercise, healthy eating, and mindfulness practices such as meditation and yoga. These habits help her reduce anxiety and improve her overall wellbeing.

Reconnecting with Her Identity: As she moves forward, Monica takes the time to reconnect with her identity outside of her relationship. She explores her interests, reconnects with friends from college, and participates in community events. This reconnection helps her remember who she is as an individual, independent of any relationship.

Volunteering and Giving Back: Wanting to turn her pain into purpose, Monica starts volunteering at a local women's shelter. There, she shares her story and encourages other women facing similar struggles. This experience not only provides her with a sense of fulfillment but also helps her recognize the strength in vulnerability and the power of sharing one's journey.

Forgiveness and Letting Go: Healing includes forgiving herself for the choices she made during her relationship with Johnathan. She learns to let go of the guilt and shame that had been weighing her down. Through therapy and self-reflection, she recognizes that her journey is about growth and learning, and she vows to move forward with compassion for herself.

Embracing New Relationships: As time passes, Monica opens herself up to new romantic relationships, but she does so with caution. She takes her time, ensuring that any potential partner respects her boundaries and treats her with the love and care she deserves. When she meets someone who aligns with her values, she approaches the relationship with open communication and trust.

Celebrating Progress: Each milestone in her healing journey—whether it's completing her degree, mastering a new painting technique, or helping someone else through their struggles—becomes a reason for celebration. Monica throws a small gathering with friends to acknowledge her growth and the positive changes in her life, reinforcing the support network she has cultivated.

Through these steps, Monica learns that healing is a journey, not a destination. It takes time, patience, and self-compassion, but she ultimately discovers a profound sense of empowerment. She emerges from her experience with a renewed sense of self, ready to embrace life's challenges and opportunities with courage and confidence.

Reflection and Notes

Can you relate to Monica's story? What aspects of his journey resonate with you?

      1.Key Takeaways:

- _____
_____

- _____
_____

- _____
_____

      2.Personal Reflection: How do you feel after reading this chapter?

- _____
_____

- _____
_____

- _____
_____

      3.Action Steps: What steps do you want to take in your own life to help you heal or grow?

- _____
_____

- _____
_____

- _____
_____

Personal Notes:

Chapter Two: Between Two Worlds

Sebastian was a 25yearold young man who had lived on his own since he was just 14. Both of his parents had died in a tragic car crash when he was only 10 years old, and his life had been shattered in an instant. One minute, he was a carefree kid riding in the back seat with his mom and dad, and the next, he was alone in the world—his parents' laughter silenced by the careless recklessness of a drunk driver.

After their death, no family members stepped forward to take him in. The aunts and uncles who once smiled at him during holiday dinners now looked the other way. And so, Sebastian was placed into the foster care system. There, he faced many challenges, moving from one home to the next and struggling to find a sense of safety and stability. The trauma built a wall around his heart, leaving him angry, isolated, and utterly lost.

Years passed, and as he drifted through life, he struggled to find a sense of self. Anger was the only constant, his faithful companion in a world that felt cruel and cold. He wished for an end to his pain more times than he could count, but every time, it seemed like a force greater than himself kept him alive, whispering that his time had not yet come.

One hot summer afternoon, Sebastian walked down 5th Avenue in Manhattan, shoulders slumped, thoughts heavy, when he accidentally bumped into a man. This was no ordinary man—he was tall, sharply dressed, with an air of sophistication that caught Sebastian completely off guard. For a moment, time seemed to slow. Sebastian found himself staring, unable to look away, drawn to the man's chiseled features and confident stride. The stranger offered a polite smile and continued on his way, but Sebastian remained frozen in place, heat rushing to his face, his pulse quickening.

As the man disappeared into the bustling city crowd, Sebastian's mind reeled. What was this feeling? It wasn't just admiration; it was something more, something deeper, something he had never allowed himself to acknowledge. He replayed the moment over and over in his mind, each time growing more confused. He'd never felt this way about anyone before—especially not a man. But for the first time in years, he was feeling something, and that terrified him.

That evening, Sebastian stood in front of his bathroom mirror, staring at his reflection as if it might hold the answers. "Am I gay?" he whispered to his own reflection. The words felt foreign, like they belonged to someone else. "What would my parents think if they were here? My dad would be furious.

My mom would be heartbroken." He collapsed onto the floor, his body shaking with silent sobs. He had spent years pushing down every emotion, but now they all came rushing back like a flood.

Desperate for clarity, Sebastian called Tiana, the only friend he had managed to keep through the chaos of foster care. When she arrived, he poured them both drinks, his hands trembling as he tried to find the right words. Finally, he blurted out, "Tiana, I think I might be... I think I might like men." His voice wavered, cracking under the weight of his confession. He braced himself for her reaction, but she simply smiled, a knowing softness in her eyes.

"I knew you were gay, Seb. I've known for years. I was just waiting for you to figure it out yourself." Her words felt like a punch to the gut. Sebastian's world tilted on its axis. He couldn't believe what he was hearing. How could she have known when he didn't even know himself?

For days, Sebastian was consumed by a whirlwind of thoughts and emotions. He felt like he was suffocating, trapped between the person he thought he was supposed to be and the person he might actually be. Was his attraction to men real, or was it just a result of the confusion and trauma he'd experienced over the years?

He feared he was betraying his parents' memory, disappointing them even in death.

One night, in a moment of desperation, Sebastian decided to test his feelings. He ventured into a gay bar in the West Village, heart racing with every step. The bar was dimly lit, filled with men laughing, chatting, and embracing openly. Sebastian felt like he had stumbled into a hidden world, a world he had never been allowed to see. He took a seat at the bar, nerves jangling, and ordered a Hennessy on the rocks. As he took a sip, a man sitting next to him, dressed in a crisp button up shirt, turned and said, "Rough day, huh?"

Sebastian, caught off guard, managed to make a small laugh. "Yeah, you could say that" he replied. The man smiled, and for the first time in a long while, Sebastian felt a flicker of warmth in his chest. They talked for hours, sharing stories about their lives, their struggles, their dreams. When the man invited Sebastian to a party later that evening, he hesitated for a moment but decided to go. Why not? he thought. He had nothing left to lose.

The party was nothing like he expected. It was filled with successful, confident men—some older, some younger, all living their truth without fear. As Sebastian mingled, he realized that he wasn't alone. There were others like him, people who had faced their own demons and come out stronger. The realization shook him to his core, and for the first time, he felt a glimmer of hope.

Days turned into weeks, and Sebastian and the man he met at the bar—whose name was Marcus—grew closer. They started spending more time together, and eventually, they became a couple. But despite his newfound happiness, questions still lingered in the back of Sebastian's mind. Am I truly gay? Or am I just trying to make sense of the pain I've carried for so long?

Late at night, as Marcus slept beside him, Sebastian would lie awake, staring at the ceiling, haunted by the ghosts of his past. Is this really who I am? he wondered. Or am I just broken?

Advice: Navigating Identity and Self-discovery

Embrace Self Exploration Without Judgment: Sebastian's journey is filled with pain and confusion, but he's starting to understand his true self. Self-discovery can feel overwhelming, especially when dealing with layers of trauma and expectations from the past. Allow yourself time to explore feelings, ask questions, and try new experiences without rushing to label yourself. It's okay to not have all the answers right away. Growth and understanding are gradual processes, and patience with yourself is essential.

Seek Support from Trusted Friends: Tiana's response to Sebastian's revelation was gentle and accepting, which made a difficult conversation feel safe and less intimidating. Surrounding yourself with supportive friends or loved ones can provide much-needed validation, encouragement, and comfort when facing self-doubt. Opening up may feel vulnerable, but trusted people can be valuable allies in your journey to understanding yourself.

Recognize That Healing from Trauma Takes Time: Sebastian's journey is about both discovering his identity and healing from his traumatic past. Trauma can leave deep wounds that may distort self-perception or complicate self-acceptance. Emotions and thoughts can get tangled, making it challenging to differentiate between unresolved pain and genuine feelings. Seeking guidance from a therapist or counselor can help unpack these emotions, separating past hurt from present truths, and allow for a healthier approach to identity and self-worth.

Reflection and Notes

Can you relate to Sebastian's story? What aspects of his journey resonate with you?

1.Key Takeaways:

- _____
  _____

- _____
  _____

- _____
  _____

2.Personal Reflection: How do you feel after reading this chapter?

- _____
  _____

- _____
  _____

- _____
  _____

3.Action Steps: What steps do you want to take in your own life to help you heal or grow?

- _____
  _____

- _____
  _____

- _____
  _____

Personal Notes:

Chapter Three: "The Price of Acceptance"

Alize was a 19yearold student at Howard University, a young woman of stunning beauty and undeniable intelligence. At 5'5" with rich brown eyes and a radiant dark complexion, she was the envy of many. Her skin glowed naturally, drawing compliments from those around her. Yet, what others saw as her beauty often felt like a double-edged sword to Alize. Being attractive, in her experience, didn't always come with admiration, it came with jealousy, with whispers, with judgment.

Alize had grown up feeling the sting of being treated as "less than" by light skinned women, who seemed to look down on her simply for being dark-skinned. These women would mock her, dismissing her as "ghetto trash," and targeting her for the name her mother had given her. "What kind of mother names their child after a cheap drink?" they'd say, snickering. "Was she a crackhead, or just a bad parent?" Their cruel words cut deeply into Alize, making her question her worth and the choices her mother had made.

Despite these hurtful experiences, Alize excelled in school. She studied psychology, determined to use her education to help the youth in urban communities. But no matter how well she did academically, she couldn't shake the feeling that she was seen as inferior because of her skin and her name.

One day, she had an opportunity to interview for a prestigious internship. Alize knew she was more than qualified—she had the grades, the recommendations, and a passion for her field. But from the moment she stepped into the office, she sensed the tension. The young CEO, a man who had inherited his role after his parents' passing, couldn't seem to get her name right. "Alize, like the drink?" he muttered with a smirk.

Despite her efforts to highlight her qualifications, he dismissed her with casual arrogance. When she pressed him, asking if there was something lacking in her application, he leaned back and said, "Maybe if you had a different name and were a little lighter, you might have made the cut." His words stung like a slap, leaving Alize reeling as she left the building. She managed to hold back her tears until she reached her car, but once inside, she broke down, sobbing and screaming, "Why me? I hate you, Mother! You ruined my life! I hate you; I hate you, I hate you!"

The pain of rejection followed her everywhere, like a shadow. Desperate for a reprieve, Alize joined her friends for a night out at a club. She hoped the music and dancing might drown out the hurt, but the discrimination followed her even there. When her friends were invited into the VIP section, Alize was left behind. The bouncer's cold words stung: "Not her, just her friends." Once again, she found herself on the outside looking in.

Alize internalized the rejection, convincing herself that the world saw her as unworthy. She believed that to succeed, she needed to change who she was. She started using photo filters on social media to lighten her skin, but that didn't feel like enough. She began bleaching her skin, going so far as to legally change her name to Melissa Coldwell. She was determined to reinvent herself, desperate for acceptance and tired of the judgment she faced.

But her drastic actions came with dire consequences. The skin bleaching treatments began to take a toll on her body, and after months of feeling ill, Alize received devastating news—she had developed skin cancer. Alone in her hospital bed, she realized that she had lost herself in the pursuit of acceptance, and now she was paying the price.

As she stared out the hospital window, she had a moment of clarity. She realized she had spent so much time trying to mold herself into what she thought the world wanted her to be, she had lost sight of her own worth. She cried out to God, apologizing for not valuing herself and begging for forgiveness. In that moment, she promised to find a way back to herself, to reclaim her identity, to be the person she was always meant to be.

Advice for Healing and Self-discovery

Healing and Self-Acceptance

Alize's journey to healing was long and difficult. She spent months in therapy, unraveling the layers of hurt and learning to embrace herself fully. She reached out to the community she once wanted to help, finding strength in guiding young girls who struggled with the same insecurities. She shared her story with them, telling them that their worth wasn't tied to their skin color or their name, but to their character and their heart.

Through her journey, Alize learned a powerful truth: self-love starts with acceptance, and the hardest battle is often the one within. As she began to accept herself, she found a new strength that allowed her to face the world with confidence.

A Message to You, Young Girls

To any girl reading this who feels like they are not enough, like the world is against them because of their skin, their name, or where they come from— know this: You are enough, exactly as you are. The world may try to tell you that you need to change to fit in, but the truth is, you don't need to change for anyone. Embrace your roots, your beauty, and your name. There's strength in being true to yourself, even when it feels like the world wants you to be something else. Don't let anyone take away the light that shines within you. You are seen, you are valued, and you are loved.

Reflection and Notes

Can you relate to Alize's struggles with feeling judged or overlooked?

    1.Key Takeaways:

- _____
_____
- _____
_____
- _____
_____

    2.Personal Reflection: How do you feel after reading this chapter?

- _____
_____
- _____
_____
- _____
_____

    3.Action Steps: What steps do you want to take in your own life to help you heal or grow?

- _____
_____
- _____
_____
- _____
_____

Personal Notes:

Chapter Four: "Playing with Fire"

Sierra always dreamed big, but her path was a rocky one, paved with her own insecurities and an untrustworthy nature that chased away anyone who got close. Since childhood, Sierra struggled to feel comfortable in her own skin, an unease that bloomed into a need to compete with every woman she met. She craved the feeling of standing out, but her confidence was often confused with desperation. When her friends introduced her to new people, she saw it as a chance to win attention. And her friends' boyfriends? They were no exception. In her constant search for validation, she often flirted with them, unable to resist the thrill of capturing another man's interest, even if it meant crossing lines. But those moments of satisfaction were fleeting, leaving her with little more than severed friendships and the kind of isolation that gnawed at her insides.

At 27, Sierra met Jenn, and something about this friendship felt different. Jenn was a magnetic personality, a social media influencer with over a million followers and a seemingly endless circle of high-profile connections. Unlike anyone Sierra had met, Jenn didn't feel threatened by her boldness. Instead, she welcomed her with an open heart, introducing her to her friends and inviting her into a world Sierra had only dreamed of. Jenn's confidence seemed effortless, and the more time Sierra spent around her, the more she envied her friend's freedom. She found herself admiring Jenn's life, wanting to emulate her—yet unable to shake the need to compete, a buried instinct that seemed ready to erupt.

Their friendship grew quickly, and for a moment, Sierra felt like she had finally found someone who saw her worth. But beneath the surface, Sierra's insecurities simmered, fueled by her longing for the life Jenn had. Her craving for attention, especially from men, lingered, and she could feel it threatening to ruin this bond she had begun to treasure.

One evening, Jenn invited Sierra to a high-profile party, an intimate gathering of influential personalities from the industry. Sierra could barely contain her excitement. This was the kind of exclusive event that defined Jenn's life, the kind of opportunity Sierra had always yearned for. The day of the event, Jenn mentioned her outfit—a designer piece meant to impress but understated enough to reflect her signature style. Sierra, desperate to stand out, went to the same store and chose something in a similar style, only louder. She wanted to be noticed, to leave an impression just as lasting as Jenn's.

When they arrived, the air was thick with glamour and whispers of exclusivity. Jenn's boyfriend, Sean, a well-known actor, approached them as they entered, his smile lighting up as he wrapped his arms around Jenn. Sierra watched as Jenn laughed in his embrace, feeling a pang of longing mixed with envy. When Sean looked up and noticed her, Sierra held his gaze for a moment too long, her eyes lingering on him with an intensity that wasn't lost on either of them.

As the night wore on, the drinks flowed, and laughter echoed through the lavish hall. The guests danced, laughed, and mingled, all while Sierra's focus drifted between the crowd and Sean. Eventually, Jenn excused herself to the bathroom, leaving Sierra alone with him. Fueled by a mix of alcohol and her own desperate need to feel seen, Sierra found herself walking over to Sean. She felt a thrill coursing through her, the kind that ignited her every time she tested boundaries.

"Enjoying the party?" she asked, her voice soft but suggestive. She let her hand rest briefly on his shoulder, the touch lingering just a little too long. Sean stiffened, glancing at her hand and then back at her with a look that was half surprise, half discomfort. He shifted, trying to create some distance, but Sierra leaned in closer, her flirtatious smile unmistakable.

Sean moved away abruptly, his expression hardening as he excused himself to find Jenn. For the rest of the night, he kept his distance, making sure to stay out of Sierra's reach. She tried to shake off the encounter, telling herself it was harmless, that he'd misunderstood her intentions. But deep down, she knew she had crossed a line, and a thrill of danger mixed with shame settled in her chest.

The next day, Sierra invited Jenn over, framing it as a casual girls' day to recap the previous night's events. As they sipped wine and laughed, Sierra decided to take control of the story, planting seeds of doubt about Sean's character. She described an encounter where she hinted that Sean had been "friendly," making sure to portray herself as uncomfortable, as though she was warning Jenn out of loyalty.

Jenn's laughter faded, her brows knitting together as she listened. She took in Sierra's words, but an unease lingered in her gaze. Knowing Sean's character, Jenn found it hard to believe her friend's claims. So, she picked up her phone and called him, pressing him about the night before. His voice was calm as he recounted the evening, telling her about Sierra's advances and how he had distanced himself. As Jenn listened, her heart sank. She knew her boyfriend, knew his values, and his account aligned with what she had seen herself. A knot of betrayal tightened in her stomach.

Jenn put down her phone and looked at Sierra, her eyes sharp with disbelief. "Why would you lie to me?" she asked, her voice low and hurt.

Sierra tried to laugh it off, shifting blame, claiming Sean had "misunderstood" her actions. But Jenn's icy stare told her it was too late. All the excuses in the world couldn't bridge the chasm that Sierra's insecurities had created. Sierra could feel the weight of her friend's disgust, the cold realization that she had finally pushed too far.

With nowhere to hide and the last bridge burned, Sierra felt a new kind of loneliness settling over her— a hollowness that came from knowing she had lost one of the few real connections in her life. As Jenn stood up, she didn't say goodbye. She simply turned and walked away, leaving Sierra alone with the wreckage of her choices.

Reflecting on Sierra's Journey:
Insecurity and jealousy are dangerous forces. They can lead us to make choices that break bonds we desperately need. Sierra's need for validation blinded her to the value of true friendship, and in seeking attention, she lost someone who truly cared for her. This chapter serves as a warning about the consequences of unchecked insecurities and reminds us that friendship, love, and trust are fragile.

Respect and integrity are essential; once trust is broken, it can be impossible to regain.

Reflection and Notes

Think about a time when you felt insecure or jealous. How did you handle it?

   1.Key Takeaways:

   - _____
     _____

   - _____
     _____

   - _____
     _____

   2.Personal Reflection: How do you feel after reading this chapter?

   - _____
     _____

   - _____
     _____

   - _____
     _____

   3.Action Steps: What steps do you want to take in your own life to help you heal or grow?

   - _____
     _____

   - _____
     _____

   - _____
     _____

Personal Notes:

Chapter Five: The Price of Fame

Marcus grew up in a world where many could only dream of—a nice home in a quiet, gated community, with parents who poured love, guidance, and resources into his life. His father was a lawyer, well respected in their city, while his mother owned a boutique that was a staple in their neighborhood. He never went without, and his childhood was filled with vacations, private school, and access to every opportunity his parents believed would shape him into a responsible, successful adult. But, like many teenagers, Marcus was lured by a world his parents could never have imagined.

It started innocently enough. On his sixteenth birthday, Marcus's parents gave him a brand new smartphone. Social media was a natural escape for him—an endless stream of music videos, flashy influencers, and the raw energy of the drill music scene. He was captivated. The passion, the gritty realism, the swagger of drill rappers drew him in, and it wasn't long before he wanted to create that same feeling. In his room, with his headphones blasting and phone in hand, he watched video after video, studying their every move. For the first time, he felt a powerful connection to something he hadn't felt in his own quiet, orderly world.

In Marcus's eyes, these rappers had it all: respect, loyalty, a hard edge that made them seem untouchable. It didn't take long for him to decide—he wanted to be a rapper, too. Not just any rapper, but one who could tell stories that people respected. So, he started writing lyrics, practicing in his room, mimicking the style and lingo he saw in his favorite drill tracks. But as he dove deeper into the scene, he realized that it wasn't enough to simply sound the part. He'd need to look and act the part, too.

With his family's financial support, Marcus had what many kids didn't. He used this advantage to start buying flashy clothes, chains, and even rented luxury cars to pose with in photos. He then began seeking out kids from the tougher neighborhoods, kids who were already entrenched in the drill music lifestyle. He showed up in places he'd only ever seen from the other side of the gated walls of his neighborhood. At first, the local guys saw him as an outsider—a "rich boy" with no real experience in their world. But Marcus had a way with words and money, and over time, he started to gain their acceptance, even admiration.

The transformation was in full swing. With each passing day, Marcus dove deeper into his new identity, casting aside his old life, his family, and even his friends who didn't "get it." His popularity on social media skyrocketed as his drill songs started gaining traction.

He was living the life he'd always dreamed of, walking the streets with the neighborhood gang, feeling invincible. But with each new follower, he got closer to a world that wasn't crafted on a screen but forged in real violence and danger.

One evening, Marcus was hanging out with his friends in a part of town his parents didn't even know he visited. They were all chilling outside a local corner store, laughing and joking, when a car suddenly pulled up nearby. In a flash, the carefree mood shifted; everyone around him tensed up, eyes darting toward the car with a mix of suspicion and dread. Marcus felt the atmosphere change, but he wasn't prepared for what happened next.

Shots rang out, and everyone scrambled for cover. Marcus's heart raced, his mind blank with fear. He ducked behind a parked car, his heart pounding in his chest as he tried to process what was happening. One of his friends, a guy named Tone, who he'd started looking up to as a mentor, turned to him with a fierce look. "Yo, Marcus! Here!" Tone shoved a gun into his hand.

"Put in some work, bro!" Tone yelled over the chaos. "Show these fools who they messin' with!"

Marcus felt the cold, heavy metal in his hand, and time seemed to slow. He looked down at the weapon, his hands shaking uncontrollably. Everything he'd watched in music videos, all the swagger and bravado he'd rehearsed in front of his mirror, vanished in that moment. His friends shouted at him, their voices filled with urgency and anger. But Marcus was frozen, staring at the gun like it was an alien object.

Seeing his hesitation, Tone snatched the gun back from Marcus, muttering angrily before firing off several shots. The screams, the smell of gunpowder, and the sight of bodies scattering on the street all blended together in Marcus's mind, creating a haze of confusion and terror. When the chaos finally ended, Tone shoved the gun back into Marcus's hand. "Hold that," he said, his voice cold and unwavering.

Marcus couldn't sleep that night. He lay awake, gripped by a feeling he'd never known—a sickening, gnawing dread. He thought about telling his parents, going back to his old life, but he couldn't bear the thought of losing the respect he'd fought so hard to earn. Instead, he kept the gun hidden, trying to push the memory to the back of his mind.

Weeks passed, but the weight of that night clung to him. One day, however, that weight became too real to ignore.

There was a knock on his door early one morning, and when he opened it, he was met by police officers. His parents were confused and terrified as they watched their son handcuffed and escorted out of their pristine home, the officers reading him his rights. The news hit him like a sledgehammer: he was being charged with murder.

In the interrogation room, the detectives presented him with evidence—the same gun used in the shooting, which they had traced back to him. Despite his desperate protests, Marcus realized that his silence, his need to belong, had trapped him. He thought back to that night, the way he'd frozen, and how Tone had done the shooting. But in the eyes of the law, it didn't matter who had pulled the trigger. He'd been there, he'd held the weapon, and now he was responsible.

At his trial, his parents sat in the courtroom, devastated, listening as the prosecution painted their son as a calculating, violent young man who had thrown away a privileged life for street cred. Marcus's heart sank as the jury returned with a guilty verdict. The sentence was clear: 25 years to life.

The months following his conviction were a blur of shock and sorrow. Sitting alone in his cell, Marcus reflected on the choices he'd made, the allure of a lifestyle he'd never truly understood. He thought of his parents, the quiet stability of his childhood home, and the path he could have taken. All of it was gone now, replaced by cold bars and the inescapable reality of his decisions.

In the end, Marcus had wanted to be real; to earn the respect of a world he had only known through a screen. But that world came with a price he hadn't anticipated—a price he would pay with his freedom, his future, and the life he could never get back.

Reflecting on Marcus Journey:

Marcus had always been the kid who checked all the boxes—polite, driven, and respectful. Growing up in his well-to-do neighborhood, he had every opportunity laid out for him, and his parents had spared no effort to give him a stable, comfortable life. But the order and predictability of that world started to feel small as he got older, especially when he looked online and saw the lives of the rappers he admired. The allure of their world—raw, unfiltered, and rebellious—was like a spark igniting something he didn't even know was inside him.

He started seeing himself as someone different, a version that could command attention and respect, and he didn't care that he'd have to step far outside his comfort zone to get there.

What he didn't realize was that while he could wear the clothes, memorize the slang, and even mimic the mannerisms, he was entering a culture with roots he didn't understand, a world built on a type of survival he'd never had to face.

In his quest to belong, Marcus ignored the voice inside that warned him this wasn't him. He didn't think about the weight that came with pretending to be someone he wasn't, or that admiration from his friends came with expectations he might not be able to meet. He didn't see the boundaries between his world and theirs until it was too late—until he was handed a gun and told to prove himself in a way he never imagined. By then, he was caught between two worlds, neither of which he could truly call his own.

And that was the irony—his desire to fit into a life he wasn't built for became his undoing. He had gained all the things he'd admired from a distance—respect, popularity, and a persona tough enough to be feared. But they came with a price he never anticipated; a price that made him wish he had never strayed from the life he'd once taken for granted.

For kids like Marcus, who might feel drawn to a lifestyle they see online or in music, it's important to remember that what you see on social media or in songs isn't the whole story. Here's some advice to help you stay true to yourself and avoid the dangers of trying to fit into a world you may not fully understand:

1. Know Your Worth: You don't need to change who you are to gain respect. The friends and mentors who genuinely value you will appreciate you for your authentic self, not for how well you can imitate someone else's lifestyle. Real respect comes from staying true to your own values and being confident in who you are.

2. Recognize the Influence of Social Media: What you see on social media is often a glamorized or even fictionalized version of reality. Everyone shares their highlights but leaves out the hardships, sacrifices, and dangers that come with certain lifestyles. Look beyond the hype and remember that people rarely show the consequences.

3. Understand the Real Risks: Some environments come with challenges and risks that can change your life in ways you can't undo. Violence, crime, and gang affiliation may seem thrilling in a video, but in real life, they often end in jail time, injury, or worse. Remember that you have the power to avoid situations where you could end up with regrets.

4. Find Healthy Role Models: Seek out people who inspire you but who also live responsibly. There are artists, athletes, and community leaders who've found success without compromising their integrity or safety. Follow the paths of those who can show you that being real doesn't mean putting yourself at risk.

5. Appreciate Your Opportunities: If you're lucky enough to have a safe environment, loving family, and opportunities, make the most of them. There's no shame in having a stable background or a supportive family— that's a gift that many people wish they had. Use it to build a future that's sustainable and fulfilling.

6. Remember, Popularity Isn't Everything: Trying to be accepted or admired by certain people isn't worth compromising your values or your safety. Trends come and go, but your future is permanent. Focus on the relationships and goals that will last and keep you grounded.

7. Trust Your Instincts: If something doesn't feel right, it probably isn't. That voice inside you, the one that questions if this is really who you are, is worth listening to. Don't ignore your instincts just to fit in or impress others. Real strength is in making choices that align with who you really are.

Choosing to live authentically, and valuing your own background and beliefs, can lead to true success, the kind that doesn't come with unnecessary risks. You can carve your own path without having to imitate someone else's. True respect and fulfillment come from building a life that's genuinely your own.

Reflection and Notes

Can you relate to Marcus' story? What aspects of her journey resonate with you?

    1.Key Takeaways:

- _____
_____
- _____
_____
- _____
_____

    2.Personal Reflection: How do you feel after reading this chapter?

- _____
_____
- _____
_____
- _____
_____

    3.Action Steps: What steps do you want to take in your own life to help you heal or grow?

- _____
_____
- _____
_____
- _____
_____

Personal Notes:

Chapter Six: The Weight of a Mother's Choices

Carla sat on the worn-out couch in her cramped living room, watching the five pairs of eyes dart around the room, each one a reflection of the men she'd loved—and lost. Five children, five different fathers, and not a single one involved. The neighborhood used to call her "the Queen of the Block" back when her relationships were fresh, but now, whispers of judgment followed her every step. And worse, she knew her kids were feeling it too.

Raising five kids on her own was a challenge, but it wasn't just the bills or lack of time. Each child was tied to a man who, at some point, had meant everything to her. And yet, here she was, left alone to navigate it all. The fathers had all moved on, abandoning her and the kids to avoid clashing with each other. And even if they had wanted to stick around, they couldn't be civil, not when they were all from rival neighborhoods, and old grudges still simmered beneath the surface. They stayed away from the kids to keep the peace, but to Carla, it only deepened the hurt.

Each child, in their own way, carried the weight of this fractured family. Junior, her eldest, had a quiet anger that she recognized in his father. He was just fourteen, but already taller than she was, with a jaw set in a way that made him look older. He'd started skipping school and hanging around the wrong corners, drawn to the streets to fill the void left by his absent father. Carla worried about him most because he was the one who saw through her excuses.

Then there was Shayla, barely twelve, yet already more mother than daughter. Carla watched as Shayla took on responsibilities that no twelve-year-old should have to. She cooked, cleaned, and looked after her younger siblings without a single complaint. Carla hated how much she relied on Shayla, but in a household this stretched, there was little choice. Shayla's father had been in and out of prison, and every time he was released, he'd show up with promises that never lasted long. Now Shayla barely mentioned him, her anger buried deep, hidden behind her caretaking and quiet resilience.

The younger three—Ty, Mason, and little Riley—were still too young to fully understand the depth of what was going on. But they could feel it. Ty's dad had left town years ago, Mason's only showed up on birthdays to drop off a few crumpled bills, and Riley's dad, well, he wasn't even on speaking terms with Carla after their messy breakup. The kids were each growing up without a steady father figure, without the structure that other families seemed to have. They were caught in a whirlwind of broken promises and fractured loyalties.

As the years passed, Carla watched helplessly as her kids were pulled further into the streets. Junior was the first. The little boy who used to cling to her leg whenever she tried to leave for work was now cold and distant, rarely home, and when he was, he stayed locked away in his room. Carla heard whispers about him getting involved with a local gang, but he brushed her off whenever she tried to talk to him about it. "I'm making money," he'd say, and she didn't know whether to feel proud or terrified.

Then Shayla changed. Once softspoken and gentle, she'd learned the tough skin her mother wore, becoming a girl who didn't trust easily, who walked the neighborhood with a hard glare, daring anyone to try her. Shayla's bond with her mother had frayed; she blamed Carla for the men she'd brought into their lives, for the fathers who never stayed.

Ty and Mason, both only a few years behind Shayla, grew up faster than they should have. Ty became known for his quick fists and mean temper, a boy who had to fight to defend his family's fractured name. Mason, quieter but no less troubled, buried himself in books, daydreaming of a way out that seemed impossible. The youngest, Riley, had been shielded from most of it, but Carla worried how long that innocence would last.

One evening, Carla sat alone at the kitchen table, surrounded by silence in a home that had once been full of laughter. She stared at the photographs scattered in front of her—pictures of birthdays, school graduations, first days of school. These moments, frozen in time, felt like distant memories from another life. Her children had grown up with gaps that love couldn't fill, scars that a mother's affection couldn't erase.

Looking out the window into the night, Carla felt the weight of her choices pressing down on her. Her children had each been loved, but they had also been left to navigate the fallout of rivalries and resentments they hadn't chosen. She had brought five lives into the world, each with their own father, each connected to a family feud and a neighborhood conflict that had nothing to do with them. Her choices had placed burdens on her children that weren't theirs to carry.

But it was too late to turn back. The streets had already wrapped their tendrils around them, luring them into lives shaped by struggle and survival. Carla had tried to keep them safe but love alone hadn't been enough to stop the inevitable pull of the world outside. She knew the streets now held a piece of each of them, shaping who they'd become in ways she could no longer control.

In the end, Carla was left in a home once filled with family but now haunted by absence. Her children had drifted away, each carving their path into the world with the tools they'd been given, limited as they were. Carla was alone, left to reckon with the choices she'd made, choices that had fractured her family and sent each of her children into the streets, each searching for something the home they shared had never provided.

As she looked at the empty rooms and silent hallways, Carla understood that the weight of her decisions had rippled outward, shaping the lives of her children, and leaving her with a family scattered and broken. And as much as she wished she could take back every mistake, all she could do now was hope that they would survive, that they would find their way in a world that had given them little mercy.

Carla had always thought she was doing her best, making decisions to protect and provide for her children, but now, looking back, she realized just how blind she'd been. Her choices hadn't only shaped her life; they had carved out paths for her children that she hadn't foreseen, hadn't guarded against. What had felt like survival at the time— finding love, seeking support wherever she could—had actually been laying down bricks in the walls her children were now forced to climb.

With each relationship, she'd hoped for stability, someone to help shoulder the weight. But her choices had drawn her children into the crossfire of rivalries and street conflicts they couldn't escape. Carla had believed that love would somehow be enough to counterbalance it all. She hadn't accounted for the simmering tensions between fathers, the estrangement of siblings connected only by blood but divided by loyalty to neighborhoods and grudges they hadn't created. She had wanted her children to feel loved and supported but hadn't seen how her decisions—her need for connection, for affection, for relief—had splintered the family she was trying to hold together.

Now, alone, Carla understood that sometimes survival isn't just about pushing forward. Sometimes, it's about knowing when to pause, to reevaluate the path you're creating, even unintentionally, for those who follow you. She'd moved forward without stopping to see the long shadow her decisions cast on her children's lives, a shadow they'd now have to step out of, one hard-earned choice at a time.

For single women in situations similar to Carla's, it's essential to recognize the long-term impact of relationship choices on yourself and, most importantly, your children. Here are some thoughts to consider:

1. Reflect on Your Relationships: Choose partners who truly add stability, respect, and support to your life. Children benefit most when they grow up around love, cooperation, and understanding. If a partner brings drama or conflict, think deeply about whether that relationship is worth pursuing.

2. Prioritize Unity for Kids' Sake: If you have children by different fathers, work to build a peaceful, respectful coparenting environment with each of them. Consistency and harmony between all parents create a stable foundation for kids. Even if the relationships didn't work out, creating an atmosphere of mutual respect with each father is one of the best gifts you can give your children.

3. Model Healthy Boundaries and Choices: Your children are watching you and learning what to expect from relationships. By showing them healthy ways to navigate relationships—respect, open communication, and positive choices—you help them build a solid foundation for their future.

4. Protect Your Children from Adult Conflict: Rivalries or grudges between fathers, or between yourself and the fathers, can become invisible burdens for your kids. Keep conflict away from your children and make sure they know

they are loved by both parents, regardless of any issues that exist between you and the other parent.

5. Prioritize Financial and Emotional Stability: Multiple relationships with multiple partners can sometimes increase financial and emotional strain. It's okay to take time for yourself and build a strong foundation before entering new relationships. Focus on what's best for you and your children before making commitments to anyone else.

6. Focus on Your Children's Wellbeing and Future: Having multiple children with different fathers can be challenging but keeping a clear vision of what's best for their growth can guide your decisions. Provide them with stability, love, and a sense of belonging that helps them feel secure and valued.

Being a single mother is tough, and there's no one size fits all approach. But being thoughtful about your choices and how they affect your children can make a world of difference for you and for them. Remember, it's about finding balance and building a future where your children feel supported, safe, and loved.

Reflection and Notes

Can you relate to Carla's story? What aspects of her journey resonate with you?

1. **Key Takeaways:**

   - _____
     _____

   - _____
     _____

   - _____
     _____

2. **Personal Reflection:** How do you feel after reading this chapter?

   - _____
     _____

   - _____
     _____

   - _____
     _____

3. **Action Steps:** What steps do you want to take in your own life to help you heal or grow?

   - _____
     _____

   - _____
     _____

   - _____
     _____

Personal Notes:

Chapter Seven: The Illusion of Acceptance

In the shimmering glow of her smartphone screen, Mariah crafted her reality. With each click, each post, she curated an image that resonated deeply with her audience—an embodiment of beauty, confidence, and allure. The world of social media was a double-edged sword for her, one that provided affirmation but also demanded constant vigilance. As a transgender woman navigating the complexities of identity, Mariah was all too familiar with the scrutiny that came with her existence.

With each filter applied and each carefully chosen caption, she created a world where she could be loved and accepted without question. Her followers adored her—an enchanting blend of glamour and authenticity, a beacon of empowerment for many. But beneath the surface, Mariah felt the weight of a facade pressing down on her, a mask that could crack under the right pressure.

Mariah had always been drawn to the allure of male attention. It was a power dynamic she had longed for, yet one that felt so often just out of reach. When she first met Kyle, it was in a crowded bar, the music pulsing like a heartbeat. He was everything she found captivating, charming, funny, with a boyish grin that could light up the darkest corners of the room. They exchanged glances that night, a silent acknowledgment of shared interest that grew into flirtation over the coming weeks.

For months, they danced around each other, both keenly aware of the electric chemistry but hesitant to dive into deeper waters. Mariah had perfected the art of seduction, knowing exactly how to allure Kyle without revealing the full truth of her identity. The thought of losing him, of shattering the illusion she had built, gnawed at her insides, but the thrill of being desired pushed her fears aside.

They spent late nights wrapped in laughter and the warmth of each other's company. Kyle adored her, captivated by the persona she had carefully crafted. The more he fell for her, the more Mariah relished the connection. Each moment felt intoxicating, a dream spun from the threads of longing and acceptance. They shared intimate encounters that intensified their bond, moments where Mariah felt most alive.

Yet, with each passing day, the truth loomed a larger shadow that threatened to eclipse everything they had built. The lies piled up, each one weighing heavier than the last, and Mariah found herself trapped in her own web of deception.

One fateful evening, while preparing for another night out together, Mariah felt a tremor of panic. She knew the time had come to confront the truth. The thought of Kyle's reaction made her stomach churn. Would he embrace her? Would he reject everything they had shared?

With a deep breath, she resolved to be honest. But as she arrived at the bar, a knot of anxiety twisted in her chest. She could see Kyle at the bar, laughing with friends, a bright smile on his face that sent a pang of affection through her. Just a few moments more, she thought, as the weight of her truth pressed heavily on her shoulders.

That night, amidst the laughter and clinking glasses, everything changed. The world around them became a blur as Mariah prepared to reveal the truth. She approached Kyle, his eyes lighting up at her presence. Yet, as she opened her mouth to speak, a moment of doubt struck her, silencing the words that had fought so hard to escape.

Days passed, and the façade persisted. But the anxiety morphed into an insurmountable dread as their relationship deepened. Mariah could no longer ignore the truth; she had built her happiness on a precarious lie.

Then came the night of the revelation. As they sat together in his apartment, the weight of their shared moments hung in the air, heavy with unspoken words. Mariah took a deep breath, ready to break the silence. But before she could gather her courage, the doorbell rang, breaking the tension.

"Just a minute!" Kyle called, rising to answer the door. In that fleeting moment, a rush of panic surged through Mariah. She glanced at her phone, heart racing—her followers were waiting for her to go live. It was a moment to share with the world, to inspire and connect, but the thought of revealing her true self loomed ominously.

Kyle returned, and the moment felt electric. "Are you okay?" he asked, concern etched on his face.

"I need to tell you something important," Mariah managed, her voice trembling. But just as she began to speak, a notification flashed across her phone screen—a live comment from her followers urging her to go live.

The pressure overwhelmed her. "Can we do this later?" she asked, desperation creeping into her tone.

He nodded, but Mariah felt a sinking dread. She wasn't just dodging a conversation; she was dodging the truth.

That night, she went live, showcasing the confidence that had become her armor. But beneath the surface, the unease churned. She could feel the distance growing between them, a gap formed from unacknowledged truths.

Days turned into weeks, and the cracks in their relationship deepened. Kyle began to notice the inconsistencies in Mariah's story, the subtle hints she tried to cover up. The look in his eyes changed from adoration to confusion, and then to something darker betrayal.

It was only a matter of time. The day Kyle finally confronted Mariah about the truth, she knew she couldn't hide anymore. As she sat across from him, the room thick with tension, she revealed her past. His reaction was immediate and fierce—shock, anger, and heartbreak rolled into one.

"Why didn't you just tell me?" he shouted, the pain in his voice slicing through her.

"I was scared," Mariah admitted, tears streaming down her face. "I thought you could love me for me."

But it was too late; the trust had shattered. In the tumult of emotions, the love they had once shared turned sour, tainted by deception.

The following weeks were a whirlwind. Mariah tried to reach out, to apologize, to explain herself, but Kyle was gone—replaced by a void filled with resentment. Then, in an act of desperation, she attempted to reconnect with her followers, sharing her pain and the fallout from her relationship.

But the damage was done. The fallout consumed her; as Kyle's anger spread across social media, so did rumors and backlash. The fallout wasn't just personal; it became a public spectacle, one that Mariah hadn't anticipated. The world watched, judged, and whispered behind screens.

In the end, Mariah was left standing alone, a once-celebrated figure reduced to a cautionary tale. Her world of curated beauty and acceptance crumbled into chaos, and the struggle for authenticity became a painful lesson in vulnerability.

She had wanted to be loved, to be seen for who she truly was, but the very deception she thought would bring acceptance led her to a path of isolation. In the silence that followed, Mariah vowed to reclaim her narrative—not just as a symbol of beauty, but as a voice for those like her, learning to navigate the world's complexities with honesty and strength.

In a society that often condemned, she chose to rise again, seeking a truth that was all her own.

Reflection of Mariah's journey: Mariah's journey is a poignant reflection on the search for acceptance and the ways we sometimes lose ourselves in the process. Her story is one of yearning for love, for recognition, and for a sense of belonging that she had struggled to find in a world quick to judge and slow to understand. As a transgender woman, Mariah faced not only the typical pressures of social validation but also the unique challenges of living in a society that often dismisses or misunderstands her identity. In her attempt to be embraced, she crafted an image so alluring that even she began to believe it could replace her truth.

Social media offered Mariah a chance to shape her life into something aspirational, a persona that was both admired and, to her followers, untouchable. She wanted to be seen as "normal," as someone worthy of admiration and affection. But in her search for love, Mariah's deception became her downfall, transforming what could have been genuine connection into a fragile illusion. Her relationship with Kyle, built on this foundation of half-truths and unspoken fears, highlights the weight of shame and insecurity that she carried with her—fears that pushed her to hide essential parts of herself in hopes of being "good enough."

Mariah's journey shows us the dangers of self-deception and the devastating toll it can take when we can't reconcile our inner truths with the image we present to the world. Her tragedy lies not in her identity, but in her decision to mask it, to believe that her true self was somehow less valuable, less deserving of love. In concealing the truth, she robbed herself of the opportunity to be accepted for who she genuinely was.

Yet, within the sorrow of her story, there is a glimmer of resilience. The fallout forces Mariah to confront herself, to break free from the constraints of others' expectations and societal pressures. In her isolation, she begins to understand that real acceptance must start from within—that love built on authenticity is the only love that can endure. Her journey, though painful, is a reminder that the path to self-acceptance is often the hardest but also the most liberating.

For anyone who feels the need to hide who they truly are, Mariah's story is a cautionary tale: when we trade our authenticity for acceptance, we risk losing ourselves in the process. Her legacy lies in the courage to embrace oneself fully, even in a world that may not always be understood, and to seek connections that honor one's truth instead of requiring it to be hidden.

For those like Mariah, caught between the desire to be loved and the fear of rejection, here's some advice that could make all the difference:

1. Honor Your Truth

Hiding who you are may seem easier in the short term, but it's a heavy burden to carry. If you want to build meaningful connections, start with honesty—about your identity, your past, and your journey. People worth having in your life will respect and appreciate the courage it takes to be real.

2. Know Your Worth Beyond Validation

Seeking validation from others is natural, but real validation comes from within. Work on building self-acceptance and self-love. Know that you are worthy of love as you are, without needing to reshape yourself to fit someone else's mold or standards.

3. Find Supportive Communities

Seek out people and spaces where you can be yourself openly and without judgment. There are countless people who understand your journey and will uplift you for who you are. Being surrounded by support can ease the fear of rejection and help you feel less alone.

4. Be Upfront with Partners

If you're dating, have those honest conversations early. While it can be daunting, sharing your truth can bring you closer to finding someone who genuinely sees and accepts all of you. Relationships based on authenticity are much stronger than those rooted in secrecy.

5. Remember the Risks of Deception

Concealing parts of yourself may seem like a way to protect yourself, but deception often leads to deeper pain. People deserve the truth, just as you deserve to be known fully. Trust that being honest will protect you more in the long run.

6. Build Self-Confidence

Confidence comes from being grounded in who you are. Invest time in your passions, talents, and personal growth. When you feel proud of yourself, it becomes easier to be open and to care less about the judgments of others.

7. Seek Professional Support if Needed

Sometimes the journey of self-acceptance and overcoming fear requires more than willpower alone. Therapists, support groups, and mentors can provide invaluable guidance, helping you to process feelings, fears, and experiences constructively.

8. Protect Yourself

Not everyone will be accepting, and some may react poorly to your honesty. Trust your instincts and take precautions when sharing vulnerable truths, especially with new people. It's okay to be selective with whom you allow into your life.

9. Remember That You Deserve Happiness

Living authentically isn't just about avoiding negative consequences, it's also about allowing yourself to experience true happiness. Embracing who you are and sharing that openly can lead to a richer, more joyful life than one built on concealment.

Your journey is your own, and being yourself fully will empower you to find people who celebrate you. It might take time, but you're worth that wait, and so is the happiness that comes with it

Reflection and Notes

Can you relate to Mariah's story or even Kyle's? What aspects of her journey resonate with you?

1.Key Takeaways:

- _____
  _____
- _____
  _____
- _____
  _____

2.Personal Reflection: How do you feel after reading this chapter?

- _____
  _____
- _____
  _____
- _____
  _____

3.Action Steps: What steps do you want to take in your own life to help you heal or grow?

- _____
  _____
- _____
  _____
- _____
  _____

Personal Notes:

Chapter Eight: The Price of a Secret

The idea for the trip came up one late Saturday night. Four old friends—Marcus, Todd, Brian, and Darnell—all married with families, were talking about needing a break from the daily grind. That's when Jay, their single friend, mentioned his recent solo trip to the Dominican Republic. "Bro, you have no idea. It's paradise," he'd said, with a grin that told stories he didn't share in full.

The idea settled in, and within a few weeks, flights were booked. They packed their bags, ready to indulge in the beaches, the nightlife, and maybe even the freedom that came from leaving behind responsibilities and expectations.

The Arrival in Paradise

As they landed in Punta Cana, the warm air hit them, and their spirits lifted. The plan was simple: relax, drink, hit the beach, and enjoy themselves. They checked into their hotel, each man slipping into the easy, carefree energy of a tropical vacation. For the first day, they kept it tame— exploring the local bars, having drinks by the beach, and sharing laughs they hadn't had in a while.

But by the second night, things took a different turn. Jay, the single friend, had a reputation for pushing limits, and he coaxed the others to join him in the vibrant nightlife. Clubs were pulsing with energy, music filled the air, and the drinks flowed freely. That night, they met a group of local women who danced with them, laughed with them, and pulled them further into the thrill of the night.

The Crossing of Boundaries

Marcus, Todd, Brian, and Darnell had always been loyal husbands, but something about the carefree atmosphere—and the influence of Jay's single lifestyle—had them lowering their usual guard. They justified their behavior as harmless fun, something they could tuck away as just a wild memory of a trip with the guys. But as the night went on, lines blurred, and promises made at home seemed a distant memory.

Jay, who had always been the one to live on the edge, encouraged them to loosen up. One by one, they were drawn in by the women they'd met, and, against their better judgment, each one eventually went their own way. A night turned into several, and while each man tried to play it cool, there was an unspoken sense that they were all pushing their boundaries in ways they hadn't before.

The Consequences Begin to Surface

Back at home, life resumed, but each man was haunted by the trip, especially Marcus. He was usually the one with a level head, but his judgment had slipped overseas, and now he couldn't shake the feeling that something was wrong. Weeks passed, and he began to feel ill sweats at night, constant fatigue, and a persistent sore throat he couldn't shake.

A visit to the doctor confirmed his worst fear. The diagnosis: HIV. The weight of it hit him hard, and he felt the walls close in as he thought of his family, his wife, and the life they'd built together. He'd made a reckless choice in a single moment, and now he was carrying a burden that he couldn't easily shake.

A Web of Lies

He felt trapped, unsure how to break the news to his friends, let alone his family. Guilt and shame ate away at him, and he tried to manage the growing secret on his own. But Marcus knew he couldn't carry the weight alone forever. He needed to tell someone to come clean to the people who'd been there with him that night.

Gathering the courage, he called Todd, Brian, and Darnell to meet up. When they were finally together, Marcus's face was pale, and his hands shook as he explained. The revelation left them silent, each man grappling with the possibility that they, too, could have been exposed. As the news sunk in, anger, fear, and panic surfaced.

"How could you not tell us sooner?" Brian asked, his voice shaking. Darnell looked at him in shock, his mind racing at the idea of facing his wife, of possibly bringing home something that could tear his family apart.

Jay sat back, stunned but unaffected. "You guys act like it's the end of the world. You knew what you were getting into," he said, brushing off the severity of the situation. His detachment only fueled the tension in the room, making them realize how his carefree attitude had pushed them toward a mistake they couldn't undo.

The Fallout

The weeks that followed were some of the hardest any of them had experienced. Brian and Darnell went to get tested, and the anxiety weighed heavily on them as they awaited the results. Todd, too, found himself constantly thinking about the choices he'd made that night, wondering if he had put everything he loved at risk.

Marcus eventually had to break the news to his wife. The conversation was agonizing, filled with tears, anger, and betrayal. She packed her things and left, taking their children with her, leaving Marcus to face the reality of his choices alone. His life unraveled as he realized that a single moment had cost him everything he held dear.

One by one, his friends felt the effects of that night ripple through their lives. Marriages were strained, trust was broken, and what had once been a close group of friends splintered under the weight of guilt and resentment. The trip that had started as an escape from routine had become a haunting reminder of the cost of impulsive choices.

The Lesson Left Behind

For Marcus, the hardest part wasn't just losing his health but the realization that he had let down everyone who mattered to him. The thrill he'd chased had left him with a life-altering consequence that served as a constant reminder of his mistakes. He learned too late that boundaries exist for a reason, and that crossing them, even for a moment, can leave scars that last a lifetime.

And for his friends, the lesson was a sobering one as well. They were forced to confront the pressures they'd allowed to sway them, recognizing how quickly temptation had led them down a dangerous path. They'd lost a piece of their friendship, and in some cases, their families, and were left to rebuild their lives from the wreckage.

The trip that was meant to be an escape had become a tragic turning point, marking a loss of innocence and a harsh awakening to the cost of recklessness. None of them would ever be the same, each bearing the weight of their choices, each scarred by the price of a secret they wished they could take back.

Reflecting on Marcus Decision making: Marcus's journey is a sobering reminder of how unchecked desires can cloud judgment and lead us down destructive paths. In the glow of the Dominican nightlife, he let himself be swayed by the thrill of temporary pleasure, forgetting the responsibilities and commitments he had back home.

The allure of the moment, the excitement of breaking routine, and the promise of adventure all whispered louder than the voice of reason and the values he'd lived by.

Marcus allowed lust to take the wheel, steering him toward choices he would have otherwise avoided. It's a harsh truth that in pursuit of instant gratification, people can lose sight of the bigger picture—the people they love, the goals they've set, and the lives they've built. His decisions were impulsive, based not on thoughtfulness or self-control but on a desire to feel free and uninhibited, if only for a night. But that single choice opened a door to consequences he wasn't prepared to face, revealing how one moment can change everything.

Marcus's actions serve as a painful example of how easily lust can distort perspective, turning fleeting excitement into life-altering consequences. It's a lesson in understanding that boundaries and self-control aren't restrictions; they're safeguards, ensuring we protect the things and people we value most. For Marcus, realizing this came too late, but his story offers a powerful reflection for anyone tempted to trade their future for a fleeting moment of pleasure.

For men like Marcus, taking trips overseas for adventure and excitement, it's crucial to keep in mind that while travel can be thrilling, safety, respect, and self-control should always be top priorities. Here's some advice for staying grounded and avoiding costly mistakes:

1. Stay Grounded in Your Commitments: Remember the relationships and responsibilities you've left at home. A trip might feel like a chance to escape, but no vacation is worth jeopardizing your family, career, or health. Keeping your commitments in mind can guide better decisions.

2. Think Long-Term, Not Short-Term: While it's easy to get swept up in the excitement of new places and people, remember that temporary pleasures can lead to long-lasting consequences. The thrill of a moment can never outweigh the impact it may have on your life and health.

3. Health and Safety First: If you're meeting new people, prioritize your health. Protect yourself by using protection if you engage in intimate encounters, and avoid risky situations that could lead to harm. You owe it to yourself to keep your health intact.

4. Stay Within Your Boundaries: It's easy to feel invincible while traveling, but that mindset often leads to poor decisions. Remember the values you live by at home, and let them be your guide, even on vacation. Don't let the thrill of being in a new place cloud your judgment.

5. Think Beyond Yourself: If you're married or in a relationship, remember that your actions affect not only

you but also those who trust you. Being responsible means respecting the people who matter to you, even when they're not around.

6. Choose Friends Wisely: Trips are often shaped by the company you keep. Surround yourself with friends who share your values and who won't encourage you to make risky choices. A good support system helps everyone stay accountable.

7. Take Time to Reflect: Before making any decision, take a moment to think about the potential consequences. A bit of reflection can keep you from making impulsive choices that may have serious repercussions.

While it's possible to enjoy a fun, memorable, and meaningful trip, staying grounded and making smart choices will ensure your travel doesn't come with unnecessary regrets.

Reflection and Notes
Can you relate to Marcus' story? What aspects of his journey resonate with you?

1. **Key Takeaways:**
   - _____
   _____
   - _____
   _____
   - _____
   _____

2. **Personal Reflection**: How do you feel after reading this chapter?
   - _____
   _____
   - _____
   _____
   - _____
   _____

3. **Action Steps**: What steps do you want to take in your own life to help you heal or grow?
   - _____
   _____
   - _____
   _____
   - _____
   _____

Personal Notes:

Chapter Nine: The Successful Bum

From outside looking in, Donovan was the epitome of success. Sharp suits, a gleaming luxury car, and a penthouse with a panoramic view of the city. He was the guy everyone envied—driven, wealthy, and perpetually single. But beneath the surface, Donovan was hollow. He wasn't driven by passion or love; his motivation was power, control, and the thrill of conquering the next woman. To him, relationships weren't about connection, they were transactions.

Donovan had mastered the art of attraction but knew little of love. He could wine, dine, and impress any woman who crossed his path, but he never stayed around long enough to let anyone truly know him. Women were like trophies, collected and forgotten once the allure faded. And because he had wealth on his side, he rarely faced rejection. Yet, in quiet moments alone, he felt the weight of his emptiness. No amount of money or adoration seemed to satisfy him. He'd grown accustomed to filling his void by flaunting his wealth and power, a hollow ritual that only deepened his loneliness over time.

Then he met Amara.

Amara was everything he thought he wanted: beautiful, sharp, and independent. She didn't seem impressed by his car or his wallet, which intrigued him even more. Unlike the others, Amara didn't eagerly accept his gifts or swoon over his lifestyle. She was kind, confident, and seemed uninterested in the material things that Donovan had come to rely on. It was refreshing, and for the first time in his life, he felt that he might have found someone who genuinely liked him for who he was.

But that's where Donovan made his biggest mistake: he assumed he was in control.

As their relationship grew, Amara seemed to unlock parts of him he'd kept hidden. He started sharing pieces of his past, his struggles, and even his insecurities, something he hadn't done with anyone else. He believed that, finally, he'd found someone who could see beyond his money and status. Yet, he failed to notice the subtle hints, the way Amara occasionally seemed to know too much about his past or the carefully concealed disdain in her gaze.

Donovan became reckless in his affection, convinced that Amara was "the one." He bought her gifts that cost more than most people's salaries, showered her with vacations, and even started hinting at the possibility of settling down. He believed he was winning her over, that this love was his to shape. He couldn't see the careful game being played beneath the surface.

Then, one evening, he came home to find that she was gone.

All the lavish gifts he'd bought her, the personal items she'd accumulated, her clothes, her jewelry, everything was gone. There was no note, no explanation. He tried calling her, but her number was disconnected. It was as if she had vanished from his life completely. And slowly, piece by piece, Donovan's world began to crumble.

The penthouse he had taken pride in was in foreclosure due to mismanaged finances and loans he'd foolishly taken out to fund their lavish lifestyle. His business began to falter, as clients left for competitors and investors pulled out. The friends he'd once impressed with expensive outings and gifts disappeared when the money did. He was left with nothing—just a hollow apartment and the bitter taste of betrayal.

As Donovan sank into despair, trying to piece together where everything had gone wrong, he discovered the truth: Amara was the daughter of a woman he'd wronged years ago. A woman he'd belittled and manipulated until she'd lost her job—a single mother whose life was turned upside down because of his cruelty. The job loss had driven her into poverty, and her daughter, Amara, had grown up watching her mother struggle and suffer.

He finally understood: Amara's love had never been real. It was a calculated plot, a slow, methodical takedown designed to strip him of everything he valued. She had mirrored his own tactics, using his weaknesses to unravel him piece by piece, just as he had done too so many before her.

In the end, Donovan was left alone, with nothing but the haunting realization of what he had become. His money was gone, his connections severed, and for the first time in his life, he was forced to confront himself—not as the successful man he'd once claimed to be, but as the empty shell of a "successful bum" who had lost everything to a woman he thought he controlled.

The revenge was complete, and Donovan, once powerful and feared, was now a broken man, left with only the wreckage of his own decisions. It was a punishment worse than he could have imagined: not only was he financially ruined, but he was finally forced to see himself for what he truly was—a man who had spent a lifetime trying to buy the one thing money could never give him: genuine love and respect.

Closer look at Donovan:

Donovan's personality was a complex mix of arrogance, insecurity, and misplaced values. On the surface, he exuded confidence—a polished, well-dressed man who moved through life as if he owned it. He believed success was measured by wealth and power, by the size of his penthouse and the price tags of his suits. For him, relationships were means to reinforce his status; he thought he could command loyalty and admiration with gifts and luxury, but this only revealed his inability to connect genuinely with others.

Deep down, Donovan's reliance on material things was a mask for his insecurities. He surrounded himself with a life he could control, carefully creating an image that would impress people and keep his vulnerabilities hidden. His lack of empathy and genuine care for others left him blind to the fact that real connections require more than gifts or status, they require a willingness to be seen and accepted for who one truly is.

In relationships, he was possessive and transactional, treating people based on their worth to him. If someone couldn't elevate his image or fit into his carefully constructed world, he dismissed them. This disdain for anyone he saw as "less than" only served to isolate him further, cutting him off from the human experiences he truly craved but couldn't admit to needing. His interactions were devoid of real connection because he couldn't see people as people; they were symbols of status or obstacles to his ambitions.

Ultimately, Donovan's personality was defined by a fundamental emptiness—a man so focused on his public image that he lost touch with his humanity. His downfall, orchestrated by Amara, was a painful but fitting end to a life driven by shallow motives. It forced him to confront the hollowness of his choices, leaving him with a haunting realization: he had spent his life trying to buy things that money could never deliver—authentic love, respect, and a true sense of self-worth.

Advice: How to deal with people like Donovan:

Dealing with people like Donovan—those who are superficial, transactional, and dismissive—requires a clear sense of self, healthy boundaries, and realistic expectations. Here's some advice for navigating relationships with individuals who tend to treat others based on status or superficial value:

1. Recognize Their Motivations

People like Donovan often act out of insecurity and a need for control, seeking validation through materialism or status. Understanding this can help you avoid taking their behavior personally. Their actions reflect their issues, not your worth.

2. Set Firm Boundaries

Establish clear boundaries and stick to them. People who treat others as disposable will often push limits, expecting others to tolerate disrespect. Don't be afraid to stand your ground, and protect your time, energy, and self-respect.

3. Don't Compete or Try to Prove Yourself

Avoid getting caught in a cycle of trying to win their approval or keep up with their expectations. People like Donovan might judge others based on appearance, status, or possessions. Trying to compete in their world only drags you down. Be authentic and remember that your worth isn't tied to their opinion.

4. Limit Emotional Investment

With individuals who tend to be transactional or manipulative, it's wise to limit your emotional investment.

Be friendly and professional, but don't expect emotional depth or reciprocation. Keep your expectations realistic to avoid disappointment.

5. Surround Yourself with Positive Influences

Instead of seeking validation from someone like Donovan, focus on building relationships with people who appreciate you for who you are, not for what you have. Genuine friends and connections are essential for maintaining a healthy perspective and strong self-esteem.

6. Trust Actions Over Words

People like Donovan often excel at saying the right things to get what they want. Watch how they treat others, especially those who can't "give" them anything. This will reveal a lot about their character and can guide you in deciding how much trust to place in them.

7. Don't Be Afraid to Walk Away

Sometimes, the best way to handle someone who's consistently superficial, dismissive, or toxic is to cut ties if possible. Walking away from someone who's treating you or others poorly shows self-respect and signals that you won't tolerate disrespect.

8. Focus on Your Own Growth and Values

Keep your goals, values, and standards at the forefront of your mind. Being around people like Donovan can sometimes lead to feelings of inadequacy, but remembering your own journey and purpose helps you stay grounded. Invest your energy in growth, not in impressing others.

By staying grounded, keeping your boundaries clear, and not internalizing their attitudes, you can protect your peace and build relationships with those who genuinely care about you. Real connections come from mutual respect, not status or appearance, and surrounding yourself with people who value these qualities will enrich your life far more than impressing someone like Donovan ever could.

Reflection and Notes

Can you relate to Donovan's story? What aspects of his journey resonate with you?

1.Key Takeaways:

- _____
  _____
- _____
  _____
- _____
  _____

2.Personal Reflection: How do you feel after reading this chapter?

- _____
  _____
- _____
  _____
- _____
  _____

3.Action Steps: What steps do you want to take in your own life to help you heal or grow?

- _____
  _____
- _____
  _____
- _____
  _____

Personal Notes:

Chapter Ten: Curves of Desire and Despair

Kim and Erica were best friends from childhood. They shared everything—their dreams, their secrets, their laughter, and their fears. Yet, even with their close bond, Kim couldn't help but notice a divide between them, one she never mentioned aloud but felt deeply. While Kim was slim and petite, Erica had curves that turned heads everywhere they went. Men seemed drawn to Erica in a way that made Kim feel like a shadow standing beside her, unnoticed and invisible.

For years, Kim brushed it off, telling herself she had other qualities that mattered more. But as she entered her twenties, the constant comparisons and missed opportunities weighed on her. She yearned for attention and admiration, the kind Erica received effortlessly. Then, one evening at a party, she met a guy named Leo. Leo was charming, attentive, and, most importantly, interested in her. Or so she thought.

As they got to know each other, Leo seemed fascinated by her insecurities. He'd ask about her friendship with Erica, joking about how guys were "crazy" for curvy women. His words ignited a thought that had lingered in Kim's mind for months—she could change. She could have what Erica had. She could be noticed, admired, and finally feel worthy.

After months of persuasive compliments and encouragement, Leo convinced her to consider getting a Brazilian Butt Lift (BBL). "It'll bring out the real you," he'd say, showing her photos of women who had transformed their bodies and their lives. Leo painted a picture of confidence and happiness, and Kim believed him. She saved up, ignoring Erica's subtle warnings and worried looks. Erica tried to talk her out of it, but Kim was determined; this was her chance to finally be the one people noticed.

The surgery was a success. When Kim looked in the mirror afterward, she barely recognized herself. For the first time, she felt powerful, radiant, and beautiful. Her confidence blossomed, and soon, she became the center of attention everywhere she went. Men who had once ignored her now turned their heads, approached her, and showered her with compliments. The thrill was intoxicating, and for a while, Kim felt invincible.

But her newfound popularity attracted more than just admiration. She started receiving messages from strangers on social media, followers she didn't recognize, men who seemed obsessed with her. Most of it felt harmless at first side effect of her new look, she thought. One message, though, stood out. A man named Rick, who had been messaging her for weeks, offered to take her out and show her "the good life." He seemed respectful, successful, and attentive, and when he invited her to a fancy dinner in the city, she accepted.

The night started beautifully. Rick was charming, charismatic, and lavished her with attention. But as the evening went on, she noticed something off. His questions grew invasive, personal, and uncomfortable. When she tried to leave, he convinced her to stay, promising he'd take her home. But instead of heading toward her neighborhood, Rick's car veered into an unfamiliar part of town.

Panic set in as Rick's tone shifted, his demeanor turning cold and menacing. Before she knew it, she was trapped. Over the next few weeks, Kim found herself imprisoned, her freedom stripped away. She was sold into a sex trafficking ring, where the men who came and went saw her as nothing more than a product to be used. Her life became a nightmare of constant fear, isolation, and degradation.

As days turned into weeks, she lost all hope. Her only escape became the drugs her captors gave her to keep her compliant and numb. She welcomed the numbness, a relief from the horrors she faced daily. Her dreams, her innocence, her self-worth—all of it faded as she sank further into addiction.

Months passed, and Kim's once-vibrant spirit dimmed. The confidence she had gained from her transformation was gone, replaced by a hollow version of herself. Her body, once a source of pride, had become a prison she could no longer escape. When authorities finally raided the location and freed her, she was a shadow of the woman she had once been. Her family and Erica tried to help her, but the trauma, the addiction, and the loss were too much to bear.

In the end, Kim's pursuit of acceptance and beauty led her down a dark path. She had sought validation, only to find herself ensnared by those who preyed on her insecurities. The world she had once dreamed of—a world of attention, admiration, and confidence—was a facade that hid the cruel, unforgiving reality beneath.

Reflection:

Kim's story is a harsh reminder of the dangers of valuing external validation over inner self-worth. Her desire to be noticed and loved led her to change herself in ways she couldn't foresee, attracting people who saw her as an object rather than a person. Her journey speaks to the importance of self-acceptance and the need to recognize when someone is manipulating insecurities for their gain.

If you find yourself in situations similar to Kim's, here are some important insights to help you navigate through them with self-assurance and clarity.

1. Value Yourself as You Are: Confidence and beauty truly begin from within. Focus on appreciating your unique qualities, skills, and personality. External changes can be appealing, but they are not a substitute for inner confidence. Remember, anyone who genuinely cares for you will value you as a whole person, not just for your appearance.

2. Beware of Manipulative Influences: People who focus on your insecurities, especially when it comes to physical appearance, may not have your best interests at heart. True friends and partners will encourage you to grow in ways that uplift your self-worth, rather than making you feel inadequate. Watch out for people who pressure you into making drastic decisions or use "flattery" to push their own agendas.

3. Prioritize Safety and Well-Being: Whenever you meet someone new, especially through social media, take steps to verify their intentions. Avoid being too open with strangers or meeting them in private settings. Protecting your safety is more important than impressing anyone.

4. Don't Let social media Define You: Social media often paints a distorted picture of beauty, success, and happiness. Remind yourself that a lot of what you see online is curated and filtered. Your life journey is uniquely yours, and it doesn't need to align with an artificial standard.

5. Find Healthy Outlets for Confidence-Building: Consider working on activities that build your confidence from the inside out. Pursue a passion, learn new skills, get involved in things you care about, and surround yourself with people who see your worth beyond the surface.

6. Seek Support When Needed: If you're struggling with self-esteem, reach out to supportive friends, family members, or even a therapist. Talking things through with people you trust can give your perspective and keep you grounded when insecurities arise.

7. Take Time to Heal and Grow: True beauty and confidence come from feeling at peace with who you are. Avoid quick fixes or drastic changes made solely to impress others and give yourself time to appreciate your own strengths. Embracing who you are, just as you are, can attract relationships and experiences that are genuinely fulfilling.

Kim's story highlights how easily our insecurities can lead us down dark paths if we're not careful. Embrace self-love, protect your peace, and trust that the right people will see your true value.

Reflection and Notes

Can you relate to either Kim or Erica's story? What aspects of their journey's resonate with you?

   1.Key Takeaways:
   - _____
     _____
   - _____
     _____
   - _____
     _____

   2.Personal Reflection: How do you feel after reading this chapter?
   - _____
     _____
   - _____
     _____
   - _____
     _____

   3.Action Steps: What steps do you want to take in your own life to help you heal or grow?
   - _____
     _____
   - _____
     _____
   - _____
     _____

Personal Notes:

Chapter Eleven: A Closing to a New Beginning

Growing up in the Concrete Jungle aka Brooklyn and NYC, my life was anything but easy. The streets that were once my playground quickly turned into a battleground. As a foster child, I was one of the fortunate ones—I had loving parents who raised me as if I were their own. They gave me care and protection, and they did everything they could to make me feel like I belonged. But somehow, it wasn't enough for me. There was always a part of me searching for something more, something I couldn't find within the walls of even the most loving home.

This book, The Twisted Truth, is a collection of others' lives, their battles, and the insecurities they've had to confront. Each story here holds a different piece of someone's truth, and while some deeply resonated with me, not all of them hit home in the same way. Some stories felt foreign, showing me struggles I'd never personally experienced. But even those gave me new insight, pushing me to understand just how diverse and complex our human experiences can be. The struggles may differ, but the strength required to overcome them is universal.

The Challenges That Shaped Me

I haven't shared much about my own story in this book but know this: it wasn't easy. I didn't come from privilege or security. There were days I felt broken, days I wanted to give up. I learned resilience not from textbooks or quotes, but from surviving in a world that didn't always feel like it was built for me. These streets taught me to be tough, but the people in my life—the loved ones who came and went—taught me about loyalty, heartbreak, and love.

Growing up, I faced obstacles that, at times, felt impossible to overcome. But with each setback, I found a new strength inside me. I realized that no matter how heavy life gets, there's always a way forward, always a reason to push on. It's this belief that shaped me that helped me see the twisted truths of life not as barriers, but as opportunities to grow.

The Unseen Battles: Psychological Resilience

What you won't see in these pages are the sleepless nights, the anxiety that creeps in when the world goes quiet, or the haunting questions that can keep you awake at 3 a.m. Like many others, I've wrestled with my own doubts and fears—thoughts that make you question your worth, your purpose, and your place in the world. That's the part of the story I'm saving for my next book. The untold journey of not just surviving but of enduring the mental battles that sometimes felt harder than any external challenge.

This next book will dive deeper into the mental and emotional impact of hardship. It will explore the moments where I felt as though I was losing myself, only to discover that those moments were building me up for something greater. People often talk about physical resilience, but the mind is where the real battle is fought. In my life, I've had to find ways to silence self-doubt, to battle the anxiety that sometimes felt crippling. And I want to share that journey with you, without the filters, without hiding behind any facades.

Unfiltered and Uncensored: My Truths to Come

In the next book, I'll bring you closer to the realities that I haven't yet touched on—the raw, uncut truths that shaped me. The challenges that society often expects us to endure quietly, I want to bring to light, no matter how dark or complicated they may be. Each of us carries burdens that we're often too afraid to share, and I'm ready to share mine. Because if there's one thing I've learned, it's that our strength lies in facing what we fear most.

There are chapters of my life that have never been told, moments where I felt broken beyond repair. But through those cracks, I found my own light. I want to take you there, to those raw and unfiltered places, so you can see the full picture. This isn't about creating a perfect story, it's about creating a real one, a story that resonates with everyone who's ever felt unseen or misunderstood

Looking Ahead: The Next Chapter

This isn't the end of my story. It's just the beginning. This book allowed me to share the twisted truths of others, but my own journey is still waiting to be told. My next book will be that story, the one that reveals my unfiltered life. I was a foster child who grew up navigating street life, surviving against the odds, and finding my voice. No filters. No sugarcoating. Just real life, as it was and as it is.

When my next book comes out, I promise you'll be captivated. It's going to be a ride through my uncut reality, filled with the challenges, triumphs, and raw truths that shaped me. Get ready to be pulled in, because once you start reading, you'll be stuck in your chair, eager to see what's next. Thank you for letting me share this part of my journey. The best, and the realest, is yet to come.

About the Author:

Ebonie "Eve" Smith is a dynamic and accomplished entrepreneur who has successfully ventured into several industries. Ebonie is a retired Army Veteran who has received numerous accolades for her outstanding service. Her remarkable contributions to the military have been recognized by former President Barack Obama, who awarded her a Lifetime Achievement Award.

With a bachelor's degree in business management from St. Joseph's University in Brooklyn, NY, Ebonie graduated with a 3.5 GPA, demonstrating her commitment to academic excellence. Through her books, she hopes to inspire and instill important values and life lessons in people's lives.

Ebonie's entrepreneurial spirit, passion for people, and unwavering commitment to excellence are an inspiration to all who know her.

To everyone who has taken the time to read this book, thank you for believing in me. It means the world to have your support.

I'd love to connect with you on social media! Find me at:

Instagram: @thetwistedtruthbook

If you enjoyed the book, share the love by sending a photo of yourself holding it to thetwistedtruthbook@gmail.com Don't forget to include your social media handle! Be creative, you might even be featured on my social media pages.

© 2024 copyright Ebonie "Eve" Smith. All rights reserved. No part of this book may be reproduced, stored in a retrieval system, or transmitted in any form or by any means, electronic, mechanical, photocopying, recording, or otherwise, without the prior written permission of the copyright holders.

This book was prepared by Scrilla Guerillaz Ent. & Magazine and Lux Nigra. Unauthorized use, sharing, distribution, or duplication of any content within this book without explicit permission is strictly prohibited and may result in legal action.

Made in the USA
Columbia, SC
20 November 2024

46529280R00069